KT-451-326

simple chic
flowers

conte

simple chic
flowers

jane durbridge   antonia swinson

photography by **polly wreford**

ideas for every room in your home

RYLAND
PETERS
& SMALL
LONDON NEW YORK

To Stephen, M

DESIGNER Luis Peral-A

COMMISSIONING EDITOR

EDITOR Sharon Ashmar

LOCATION RESEARCH Cla

PRODUCTION Tamsin Cu

ART DIRECTOR Gabriella

PUBLISHING DIRECTOR A

FLOWER STYLING Jane D

TEXT Antonia Swinson

First published in the
in 2003 by
Ryland Peters & Small
20–21 Jockey's Fields
London WC1R 4BW
www.rylandpeters.com

10 9 8 7 6 5 4 3

Text, design and photo
© Ryland Peters & Sm

All rights reserved. No
may be reproduced, st
or transmitted in any f
electronic, mechanical
or otherwise, without t
publisher.

ISBN 1 84172 397 5

A CIP record for this bo
British Library

Printed and bound in C

flower basics

design principles

Worry less about choosing flowers which you think will match your décor than about choosing flowers you love and will enjoy living with. If you like the way they look, that's good enough. If you're unsure where to start, use white flowers or foliage alone, either of which will look good in any interior.

A few stems are often enough to make a focal point if you choose flowers with impact such as lilies (*Lilium*), alliums (*Allium*), African lilies (*Agapanthus*), orchids (Orchidaceae family) or delphiniums (*Delphinium*). Using an odd number of stems tends to give a better effect than an even number.

Think twice before you throw out bottles, jars or anything else which could be used to hold flowers (see page 12 for inspiration).

Most of the arrangements in this book use a single variety of flower in a single colour, a method which is both simple and stylish. If you want a mixed arrangement, you can, of course, buy separate bunches and combine them yourself. If you're not that confident, try buying a ready-mixed bunch from a florist. If it's been hand tied, you've got an instant arrangement, so don't make the mistake of untying it – it'll look much better if you just put it in a container as it is.

We're spoilt for choice nowadays and many flowers are available all year round. This has obvious advantages in winter when flowers would otherwise be scarce. However, if you buy according to season, you'll get better value for money and the pleasure of enjoying things at the right time of year: daffodils (*Narcissus*) in spring, for instance, and cornflowers (*Centaurea cyanus*) in the summer.

If you're using a mixture of containers (see, for instance, the botany table display on page 104), keep one element of continuity to prevent the effect being that of a jumble. In this instance, all the bottles are clear glass and are tall and narrow. A collection of blue glass bottles, teacups, jam jars or white ceramic containers in different shapes could look equally effective.

One of the easiest ways to arrange flowers is to cut the stems so that the heads sit just above the rim of the container. This also makes a small bunch look bigger than it is.

Although you shouldn't be inhibited by any notions of flower-arranging rules, a couple of basic guidelines may help you when you're getting started. Large vases with wide necks usually need large arrangements to look their best. You'll get away with a sparser arrangement if a vase is large but narrow necked, or if it's tall but narrow. A round pot usually looks best with a full, dome-shaped bunch.

If you're experimenting with flower arranging for the first time, start with material from your garden or the less expensive bunches stocked by supermarkets so that if you make mistakes they won't be expensive ones.

Opposite **Flowers are extraordinarily versatile, lending themselves to formal, graphic treatments such as this one just as readily as they do to more relaxed schemes.** Right **As an alternative to cut flowers, many spring bulbs can be planted indoors for a colourful winter and spring display.**

vases and equipment

TO HAVE AND TO HOLD Finding the right container for a flower display is as important as the arrangement itself. With a bit of imagination, almost anything can be put to stylish use. Vases can, of course, be expensive but beautiful designer pieces should last a lifetime and can make a big statement in a room. There are, however, a host of cheaper alternatives which, with the right flowers and foliage, can look just as effective. Vintage containers have great charm and can often be picked up in junk shops or at jumble sales and car boot sales – usually fruitful hunting grounds. You may have the opportunity to rummage in relatives' attics or cupboards, and a quick scout round your own home will probably yield olive oil, water, wine, ginger ale or even scent bottles, as well as teacups, glass jars and odd tumblers. All of these can be put to creative use.

Opposite **Flower arrangements needn't involve much time or money. Here, a cylindrical vase and a few stems of ivy (*Hedera helix*) from the garden create an instant, chic result.** Right **Disguising flower stems with coffee beans transforms the look of a simple vase.**

BITTER SWEET You don't need specialist materials to create striking displays – a raid on the kitchen provided the starting point for this one. Though hardly a classic combination, chocolate-brown coffee beans and blowsy, ivory Anne Marie roses (*Rosa*) look surprisingly effective together. The contrast in texture and colour adds a touch of drama. The roses are trimmed to the height of a small glass vase (a jam jar would also work well) and grouped into a tight cluster. They're then placed in a larger, square vase and the space between the two containers is filled with beans. This vase within a vase technique can be used with many other materials, from pebbles and glass nuggets to dried pulses and even slices of fresh fruit.

Left and right **The shape of a vase often suggests a particular shape of arrangement, but there's always more than one way of displaying flowers in a vase. For instance, using long-stemmed flowers in a tall vase will look more formal than allowing their heads to spill over its rim.**

This page **A small, round pot is matched by a domed bunch of chincherinchees.**

Far right **The graphic look of this ring-shaped vase finds a good counterpart in the long, curved lines of aspidistra leaves.**

TAKING SHAPE Containers come in all shapes and sizes. Getting the right balance between the shape of your container and the shape of your flowers is a crucial element in an arrangement. For instance, the domed shape of the bunch of Turkish chincherinchees (*Ornithogalum arabicum*) shown left mimics the round pot in which they've been placed. If you've got a tall, narrow container, combining it with long-stemmed flowers – see the alliums (*Allium*) on page 86 – makes a very exaggerated, emphatic statement. However, arranging flowers so that the heads form a lollipop effect above the rim of a tall vase – see the roses (*Rosa*) on page 51 – creates a softer look. Even with very small containers such as teacups there's scope for variety: compare the single poppy anemone (*Anemone coronaria* De Caen Group) on page 83 with the tight posy of roses (*Rosa*) on page 25.

Quirky, unusual containers may inspire you to create living sculptures with your flowers, such as the tightly bound tower of narcissi (*Narcissus*) on page 56, or this ring-shaped vase, above, with an asymmetric formation of aspidistra leaves (*Aspidistra*). Large, cylindrical vases or goldfish bowls allow you to experiment with effects which are designed to be viewed *through* the glass, such as the floating cornflowers (*Centaurea cyanus*) on page 63. Conversely, arrangements in shallow containers may look most effective from above, such as the geometric green chrysanthemums (*Chrysanthemum*) on page 41. The secret is to experiment and have fun doing it.

COLOUR THERAPY A container can either contrast with or complement its contents. As this show-stopping display of parrot tulips (*Tulipa*) shows, right, some containers seem to cry out for a particular flower. Taking a different approach, the orange gerberas (*Gerbera*) on page 33 have been placed on blue-black plates for a deliberate colour counterpoint. The lilac-pink sweet peas (*Lathyrus odoratus*) in a pale green vase, left, are also a contrasting combination, but a far gentler one. For the greatest flexibility, clear glass or white ceramic are neutral backdrops which work with any colour. Galvanized pots are also versatile, while black containers add drama and usually work best with a strong colour — such as red — or, of course, white.

Above **Whether you decide upon subtle or powerful colour combinations will depend on your mood, your home's décor and what's available at the time. The great thing about using fresh flowers is the fact that they're temporary and can be replaced with a different arrangement in an instant.**
Right **Clear, white or pale containers are the easiest and most versatile to work with, suiting the whole spectrum of flower colours.**

Right **Sometimes the choice of flower determines the choice of container, but at other times a striking container will inspire an arrangement itself. Here, a spectacular vase was the starting point and the flowers naturally followed.**
Far right **Only a few pieces of inexpensive equipment are needed to create the displays in this book.**

EQUIPMENT You need very little paraphernalia to reproduce the arrangements in this book. However, a few easily obtainable items will be useful. Sharp kitchen scissors cut most plant stems and secateurs will deal with anything tougher, such as branches of blossom. Florist's wire is useful for tying and binding – see the pussy willow display on page 120, for instance – but raffia or garden twine will often do instead. Pebbles can be used in table decorations or to top dress pots (see pages 45 and 46) and can be bought from home improvement stores or garden centres. Pin holders, available from florists, are an old-fashioned but effective device for anchoring plant stems (see the gerberas on page 111). Finally, although I haven't used it in this book, florist's foam is also handy for anchoring plant stems, particularly in shallow containers.

colour
themes

yellows

SPRING SUNSHINE Dwarf daffodils (*Narcissus*), along with their larger sisters, make a welcome appearance in late winter and early spring, brightening up the garden with their cheerful flowers. Bulbs are available in garden centres or by mail order through specialist suppliers and can be planted in all manner of containers for an indoor display. For this conservatory a rich, golden yellow variety called Tête-à-tête has been grown in small, galvanized pots, top dressed with moss. Many winter- and spring-flowering bulbs can be grown indoors, among them scented paper-white narcissi (*Narcissus papyraceus*) and hyacinths (*Hyacinthus*), dwarf tulips (*Tulipa*) and irises (*Iris reticulata*), and crocuses (*Crocus*).

One type of dwarf daffodil has been grown here, but you could experiment with a mixture. There are many beautiful varieties – ranging in colour from cream to bright yellow – including some, such as geranium narcissi (see page 107), with white petals and orange cups.

This page and bottom right **Although yellow is a hot, energizing colour, it needn't be strident. In both of these arrangements, its warmth has been** tempered by the presence of cooler colours – the grey of a stone-effect pot and the blue and white of a vintage teacup and saucer.

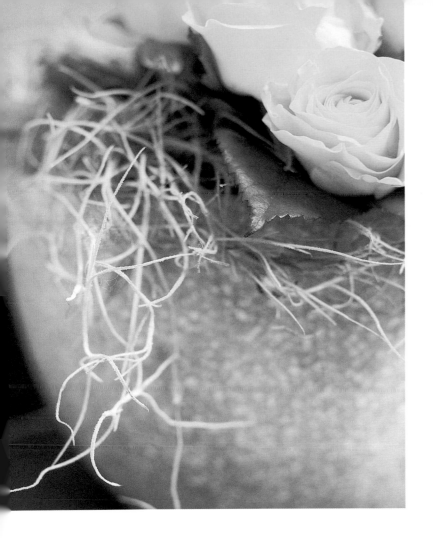

MELLOW YELLOW This pretty arrangement could be given as a present or used as a place marker at a dinner party. Yellow spray roses (*Rosa*), some opened, some in bud, have been cut short and placed in a vintage teacup and saucer. The Idea could be adapted for a small wedding reception by putting posies, tied with pretty ribbon, in guests' glasses so that they can be taken home at the end of the day as favours. If you wanted to use this type of arrangement as place markers or favours, you could experiment with variations on the theme. Using one colour of rose and one pattern of china throughout produces an elegant, coordinated look, but you could give each guest a different type of rose and teacup for an attractively eclectic effect.

A small, compact bunch of yellow roses has found a home in a stone-effect garden pot, placed by a handbasin in a bathroom. Effective flower arrangements are often as much about texture as they are about colour and here the addition of cobwebby Spanish moss (*Tillandsia usneoides*) produces a soft-focus feel. The wispy, gossamer-light moss echoes the delicacy of the rose petals themselves, making this a pretty and feminine arrangement. The cool, grey shades of the pot, which reflect the basin surround, work surprisingly well with the warmer tones of the flowers, creating a display which is pleasing and restful on the eye.

oranges

HOT FAVOURITE Sometimes you'll find a flower so irresistible that it cries out to be taken home and put on show. At other times the inspiration will come from elsewhere, and in this case it's a spectacular tall, glass vase, shaded from deep red through vermilion to tangerine. Filling it with deep orange parrot tulips (*Tulipa*), flamed with red, is a marriage made in heaven. Arranging the flowers with the heads spilling over the rim of the vase balances the height of the display and focuses attention on the intricate markings on the frilled petals. A centrepiece as big and intensely colourful as this needs the right sort of backdrop and this living room, with its neutral walls and large orange painting (by Mark Upton), complements rather than competes with it.

Tulips are an invaluable ingredient in the flower arranger's palette. They have a strong and beautiful form, last well, are good value for money and can be found in almost every colour of the rainbow – true blue being about the only exception.

Orange is a sunny colour and looks uplifting against a pristine white backdrop. With darker colours it acquires a more grown-up, glamorous air. Here, parrot tulips (*Tulipa*) in all the shades of a sunset have been placed in a shiny, black ceramic vase and provide a shot of searing colour alongside the dark furniture.

STATELY HOME Crown imperials (*Fritillaria imperialis*), left, are majestic flowers, their topknots of slender leaves above vermilion bells giving them the appearance of miniature palm trees. Placing them in a curvy, dark brown glass vase shows off their height and creates a show-stopping arrangement, even when using only five stems. Flowers as unusual as this look most effective in a room whose décor won't be overshadowed by their flair. Here, they are flanked by strong lines and colours – dark bookcases and large, masculine chairs.

Crown imperials aren't for everyone – apart from their quirky looks they have an earthy smell which some people find disagreeable. They could be replaced by blue or white African lilies (*Agapanthus*) or alliums (*Allium*, see page 87) for an equally eye-catching arrangement.

Left **It takes confidence to use flowers as tall and unusual as these in the home. However, arranged in a striking vase and placed where they'll command attention, they look wonderful.**

CITRUS ZEST For creating stunning, yet simple arrangements, gerberas (*Gerbera*) are almost too good to be true. Their large, multi-petalled blooms are pretty and open, and come in a vibrant array of colours – particularly yellows, oranges, reds and pinks. They are bold and beautiful, and last extremely well. Here, a burnt-orange variety contrasts with a dark wooden table and deep blue china to create an uncomplicated, lively display for a dinner party. A shallow vase with three separate compartments holds individual blooms, their stems cut short, with the addition of some papyrus stems (*Cyperus papyrus*), right, as an accent. More gerberas decorate the plates and a bowl piled high with ripe oranges ties the colour scheme together.

The combination of dark brown, blue and orange is a bold and sophisticated one. Orange also works well with other colours at the warm end of the spectrum, such as red and yellow, or as a foil to dazzling white.

English pot marigolds have been in cultivation for hundreds of years and possess an unpretentious simplicity which is hard to resist.

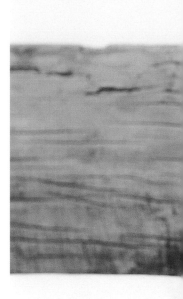

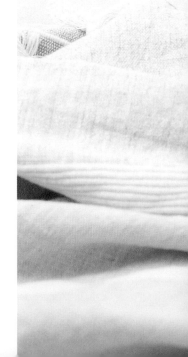

SWEET ORANGE A rough wooden bed head and cabinet set a rustic tone in this bedroom. Pot marigolds (*Calendula officinalis*) are an old cottage-garden favourite and match the mood perfectly. They are some of the easiest annuals to grow and will bloom obligingly throughout the summer. Sow a packet of seeds in the spring and you'll have enough flowers to adorn your home and garden all season. In colour, marigolds vary from cream and apricot to rich yellow and bright orange, with double as well as single forms.

Here, a small tied bunch — some of them in flower, some in bud — have been popped into a smoky-glass cube vase, along with a few of their leaves, for the simplest of arrangements. If marigolds aren't to your taste on display in the house, they may be to your taste in the kitchen — the petals are edible (as long as they haven't been sprayed) and look wonderful added to a salad.

greens

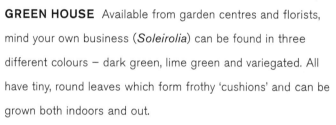

Right **Though they are traditional items of garden paraphernalia, galvanized buckets have been given a new lease of life by modern florists. This tiny one is just the right size for a frothy dome of mind your own business.**

GREEN HOUSE Available from garden centres and florists, mind your own business (*Soleirolia*) can be found in three different colours – dark green, lime green and variegated. All have tiny, round leaves which form frothy 'cushions' and can be grown both indoors and out.

In the home, mind your own business looks good almost anywhere – next to a handbasin in the bathroom, on a kitchen windowsill, lined up on a living-room mantelpiece or, as here, as an attractive addition to a dinner table. Plants in all three colour forms have been placed in small, chunky glass vases along the length of a low, wooden table. The oriental tableware and white walls reinforce the room's contemporary, minimal look and the neat green domes of leaves bring a touch of light relief to this slightly austere setting. Mind your own business, like ornamental grasses (see pages 44–45), makes a very effective table arrangement because its tactile quality invites guests to run their hands over its leaves.

whites

MODERN ROMANCE Two branches of cherry blossom (*Prunus*) say it all, heralding spring with style. This elegant and spare arrangement – housed in a tall, wood-grained earthenware vase – has oriental overtones, echoing the Japanese love affair with the cherry tree. The arching branches and their delicate white blooms are graceful and feminine, and can be found in almost any suburban garden. Branches from other trees could, of course, be used – apple (*Malus*) perhaps, or pear (*Pyrus*).

This page **Twigs from the garden, fixed to a blank wall with picture pins and reusable adhesive tack, make a new way to say it with flowers. This piece of original art was created by Laurent Bayard. Such an arrangement could be put up quickly as a surprise for an anniversary, birthday or homecoming and just as easily changed or removed. To partner it, ivory roses** (*Rosa*) – which could be substituted with peonies (*Paeonia*) or tulips (*Tulipa*) – peep over the rim of a tall, square vase.

Opposite **This painting is by Mark Upton.**

Although these two arrangements use a single type of flower, different shades of white sit very happily together. Using combinations of different white flowers in an arrangement is an easy and foolproof way to use them in the home.

PURE E

exquisite

and exc

flower

in any

which

A

mar

cor

sm

e

Tulips give their money's worth as a cut flower and provide a long-lasting and colourful show. These tulips are the classic shape we associate with them, but there are other shapes, such as parrot tulips with extravagantly frilled petals (see page 28) and lily tulips with pointed petals.

WHITER SHADES OF PALE White comes in myriad variations and can be dazzling, creamy or tinged with pink, yellow, green or blue. Opposite, these roses (*Rosa*) are a warm white with yellow and pink undertones and provide a bold contrast to a black leather-effect vase. They've been cut so that their stems can't be seen above the rim of the vase, focusing the eye on the full, voluptuous blooms. The same roses have been used to decorate place settings and sit on pieces of slate surrounded by a scattering of white pebbles, creating a look which is a mixture of oriental restraint and pure romanticism.

This page, these snowy white tulips (*Tulipa*), packed into a chunky square vase, look quietly chic in this monotone interior. Tulips change in character as their blooms age. When newly open, as here, their ovoid shape looks sleek and modern; as they open more fully, they assume a more romantic form.

Far left **The English woodland bluebell is one of the great joys of spring and suits a simple treatment such as this one.**
Left and right **The beauty of grape hyacinths' sky-blue cones of flowers is worth appreciating in close-up. This interesting technique would also work well with hyacinths (***Hyacinthus***), tulips (***Tulipa***) or bluebells.**

BLUE BELLES A little bunch of bluebells (*Hyacinthoides non-scripta*) brings spring to the kitchen, opposite. They've been popped into an enamel tea caddy and placed where their heavenly scent can be enjoyed at close quarters. Don't forget that bluebells should never be picked from the wild. There's no need to anyway – plant a bulb or two in your garden and they will multiply happily year after year.

Grape hyacinths (*Muscari*), like bluebells, are spring-flowering bulbs. The slightly magnifying effect of glass, left, brings out the intricate beauty of their tightly clustered flowers which, if they are barely opened when first cut or bought, will last for ages. A large bunch has been packed into a hurricane vase, above, with just enough water to give the plants a drink without making the leaves and stems soggy.

SWEET DREAMS Though not as long-lasting as some cut flowers, sweet peas (*Lathyrus odoratus*) more than compensate with their sheer beauty. Their delicate, ruffled petals and mouthwatering colours make them one of the most feminine and romantic flowers, and most varieties have the additional delight of scent. Opposite and inset, a bunch of lilac-pink sweet peas in a green glass vase sits prettily in a bedroom. The two colours are a contrasting combination but in shades as soft as this the effect is gentle rather than stimulating. Sweet peas are available from florists but the plants are easily grown at home from seed and look charming scrambling up a trellis or wigwam. As with all annual flowers, regular cutting will encourage more blooms and ensure a bountiful crop all summer.

Sweet peas come in a wide variety of colours, from white, pastel pinks and lilacs to bright reds, purples and purplish-black. Using a single shade, as here, produces an elegant effect, but all the colours can be combined for a less sophisticated, cottage-garden look.

LIGHT FANTASTIC Formality is a useful element in creating simple but stylish flower arrangements. This line-up of six tubular, purple glass vases and deep pink tulips (*Tulipa*) achieves its impact through repetition. Its rigidity is softened, however, by allowing the flowers to arch in different directions, creating a look which is therefore both formal and informal. The effect of light is very pleasing here, too. Reflectiveness is provided by the shiny marble mantelpiece as well as the large mirror, and the natural light is filtered subtly through the smoky glass. Placing flowers by mirrors helps to heighten their impact, not only because they're seen twice but also because they're seen from a different angle.

Right **These small, neat tulips are particularly well suited to these narrow vases because their stems are strong enough to hold the flower heads well above their rims but flexible enough to arch attractively.**

reds

This page **Arranging** flowers *inside* containers opens up all kinds of new and exciting possibilities. It's not only round bowls which can be used in this way (see pages 65 and 119 for further ideas). If callas are unavailable or beyond your budget, tulips (*Tulipa*) could be used successfully in their place (see page 98).

SPECIAL EFFECTS Opposite, coiled around the inside of a goldfish bowl, these calla lilies (*Zantedeschia aethiopica*) do indeed look like a shoal of fish. Here, the stems play as important a role as the flowers, creating an intricate pattern against the glass.

Carnations (*Dianthus*) are a mainstay of the floristry business, and no wonder: they last for ages, are inexpensive, are available all year and come in a fabulous range of colours. Because they're so widely available, they've suffered from being overused. However, this display – three pumpkin-shaped candles, each filled with a little water and a dome of carnations – shows how pretty they can look.

BOLD AND BEAUTIFUL Left, for a bit of pure, irreverent fun, a small bunch of exuberant glory lilies (*Gloriosa superba*) has been popped into a kitsch Pink Panther toothbrush holder. This tongue-in-cheek approach reflects the replacement of rigid rules in flower arranging with a more relaxed approach.

Below, in a variation on the goldfish-bowl theme (see page 96), red tulips have been wrapped around the inside of a shallow bowl. An arrangement like this will provide new interest every day because tulips continue to grow in water after they've been cut, producing a changing, living display. Bright red isn't an obvious choice for a bathroom, but against the pristine white handbasin and tiles it strikes a vibrant and energizing note.

Opposite, strong red can be a bit overwhelming if used on its own. The splashes of white on the petals of this pretty dahlia (*Dahlia*) lighten its effect, as do the green buds emerging from the bunch. Choosing variegated flowers is a useful ploy for anyone who wants to experiment with bold colour without going the whole hog.

Passionate and intense, red isn't a colour for everyone. Used judiciously, however, it can be both warming and uplifting – a good choice for those moments when you need a lift.

Despite the fact that roses are available in a vast array of colours, many as intense as this shade of red, commercial growers have gone one step further and produced fresh, dyed roses in brilliant colours – including electric blue – which can be found at certain florists.

ROLE REVERSAL Giving flowers as a love token is an age-old practice, and roses in particular have been linked with romance since ancient times. Valentine's day and red roses go hand in hand, but giving flowers needn't be the exclusive preserve of men. This dashing bouquet was designed with a man in mind, a new twist on the classic bunch of a dozen red roses. A copy of the *Financial Times*, tied with a masculine flourish of black raffia, replaces the usual wrapping paper or cellophane – and does double duty as useful reading material! It's not hard to see why roses remain the queen of cut flowers – available all year, everywhere from florists to supermarkets and garage forecourts, their range of colours is second to none and they last extremely well in arrangements.

vibrant
combinations

Pinks, blues and purples work harmoniously together, particularly when they're at the paler end of the spectrum. They're the quintessential colours of an English summer garden and suggest femininity and old-fashioned romanticism.

SWEET PASTELS Soft pinks and blues combine easily and are restful on the eye, making them a good choice for a place of relaxation such as a bedroom. These blue cornflowers (*Centaurea cyanus*), catmint (*Nepeta*) and ice-cream pink roses (*Rosa*) look pretty and feminine in a white porcelain fifties vase on a bedside table. The arrangement is simple but it has a touch of formality, making it refined and ladylike.

Opposite, inspired by memories of the botany table at school, this series of deliberately mismatched vases and bottles is filled with single stems of wild and garden flowers. Among them are dill (*Anethum graveolens*), African lily (*Agapanthus*), sea holly (*Eryngium*), roses (*Rosa*), herbaceous sage (*Salvia*) and Virginia creeper (*Parthenocissus quinquefolia*). The result is rustic and charming and can be achieved with minimum effort and cost.

HOUSE WARMING Reds and pinks don't always work well together, but this bunch of ranunculus (*Ranunculus asiaticus*) shows how rich the effect is when they do. Ranunculus are often available from florists in mixed bunches, making easy work of deciding which colours to put together. Here, the flowers have been loosely arranged in a tall white vase on a bedside table and look fresh and summery against the room's pristine white décor. A simple red-and-white striped cushion adds a complementary touch of colour.

Opposite, yellow is the colour we all associate with daffodils (*Narcissus*) but this dwarf variety, called geranium, has white outer petals and a deep orange-red cup. A book cover combining orange and red inspired the choice of container for the arrangement – a red glass vase. The combination is warm and uplifting, just right for the time of year when winter's dark days are giving way to spring.

Opposite **There's nothing wrong with letting a florist do some of the work for you and buying a ready-made bunch of flowers, such as these mixed ranunculus.**

This page **You may find inspiration where you least expect it – here, a book cover suggested this combination of narcissi and a red glass vase.**

SUN SHADES With their fine, papery petals, Iceland poppies (*Papaver nudicaule*) look fragile and, indeed, they have a short lifespan as a cut flower. However, they make up for this lack of staying power with their gorgeous sunny colours, usually a riotous mixture of yellows, oranges and reds, often tempered by white. They also have a very graceful form, their hairy stems bending over under the weight of their large blooms. For one arrangement the flowers have been put in a tall, red glass vase; for the other a dark-grey glass vase has been used. Whatever you choose to put them in, the result will be cheerful and welcoming — a glimmer of sunshine in any room.

Iceland poppies
require a very
particular and
unusual method
of conditioning if
they're to be used
as cut flowers: the
bottom of the stems
need to be seared
with a match.

This page **It's not just their sunny colours which make gerberas such cheerful flowers to have around the home; their large, open blooms also strike a positive note.** Opposite **Using a cocktail of strong colours requires confidence but the results can be uplifting, especially when set against the neutral backdrop of a white wall.**

BRIGHT SPARKS This display of mid-pink and sunny yellow gerberas (*Gerbera*) couldn't be easier to create. Glass phials, now widely available, can be stuck onto a wall where the flowers can be enjoyed at close quarters – by the kitchen sink, as here, or perhaps on a bathroom mirror. Since few stems are used, the flowers can be changed regularly at minimal cost. Gerberas come in a host of cheerful colours but poppy anemones (*Anemone coronaria* De Caen Group), carnations (*Dianthus*) or any other favourite flower could be used.

Opposite, more vibrant gerberas, this time arranged in a fifties steel bowl with a black exterior and red enamelled interior. Rather than cutting the stems level with the rim of the bowl, they have been left long and anchored with the use of a pin holder to give the display a more structured look.

RICH PICKINGS If you're unsure how to combine colours yourself, it's simpler to buy a bunch which does the job for you. Opposite, these tightly furled ranunculus (*Ranunculus asiaticus*) in rose and bright pink, orange, red and yellow form a summery mass of colour and show how well these warm shades work together. The flowers have been cut to a uniform length and arranged informally in a simple white china bowl. Chicken wire, scrunched into a dome, was placed in the bowl and secured with adhesive tape to create a framework to hold the stems. With a small bowl, you may need a pin holder or weight in the bottom to act as ballast so the flowers don't make it top heavy.

Above and above right, a bold arrangement of sunflowers (*Helianthus annuus*), lotuses (*Nelumbo*) and cordyline leaves (*Cordyline*) doesn't compromise the masculinity of this bedroom. Hot pink and deep yellow are a punchy combination and create a hot spot of colour in this subdued interior.

Combining warm colours produces a positive and vibrant effect. However, if you're wary of putting this sort of scheme together yourself, you can begin by buying a ready-made bunch from a florist. You may then feel confident enough to create your own delicious floral medley.

SUMMER ON ICE An ice bowl makes a spectacular dinner party centrepiece and isn't as hard to make as it looks. Take a plastic or Pyrex bowl and place a smaller one inside it, then stick adhesive tape across the top of both bowls in a crisscross pattern, making sure that the rims of the bowls are level. Tuck flowers, leaves or fruit down the gap between the bowls and carefully fill with water, then freeze. Here, sprigs of rosemary (*Rosmarinus officinalis*) not only look good but help to anchor smaller items such as the pink and red rose petals (*Rosa*), which might otherwise float to the top. Summer berries – which also look pretty frozen into an ice bowl – have been piled inside for a delicious dessert. Dark pink tulips and glassware match the sumptuous colours of the berries and help to create a table setting guaranteed to make mouths water.

A gorgeous colour palette of tempting berry shades helps to set the scene for a beautiful summer feast. Ice bowls look impressive but are simple to make once you've mastered the basic technique.

naturals

Above **Echeveria** (*Echeveria*) can be bought at garden centres. Here, they've been split into individual rosettes and their roots washed of soil. They've then been placed in small, plain glasses to create an indoor water garden on a low table. When it's time for a change, a home can be found for the plants in the garden.

NATURAL SELECTION Many shrubs require pruning in the autumn or winter. Instead of consigning the resulting pile of branches to the bonfire, keep the best and put them to stylish use. Opposite and top left, a half-metallicized earthenware vase holds an arrangement of bare branches whose intricate tracery is highlighted by the neutral background. This is the ultimate in low-maintenance floristry: you don't need to add any water to the container and the result will last all winter.

Above, this collection of pebbles, candles and plants on a mantelpiece makes a beautiful still life. The smaller vase holds St John's wort berries (*Hypericum*). Ivy (*Hedera helix*) has been coiled inside the cylindrical vase and pears placed in the bottom.

SPRING STILL LIFE Pussy willow (*Salix caprea*) comes into flower in spring and is a familiar sight in the countryside, although it can also be bought in florists. The stems, covered in trademark furry nodules, are supple enough to be bent and coiled, giving the idea for this sculptural display.

A bunch of long stems, bound at the base with florist's wire and anchored using a pin holder, has been placed in a square aluminium dish. More stems have been coiled into a circle and secured with florist's wire. As an optional extra, a few heads of dyed yellow amaryllis (*Amaryllis*) have been tucked into the display to add a touch of vibrancy. Placed on a low coffee table, the stems have a simplicity reminiscent of oriental flower arrangements.

Right **Fresh, dyed flowers, such as these yellow amaryllis, can be bought at some florists. The technique involves submerging cut stems in dye, which is drawn up by the plant to tint the petals. Dyed flowers are often very bright colours, so they're useful for times when you want to make a bold statement or just have a bit of fun.**

flower care and conditioning

• When you're buying flowers, take the time to make sure that those you're choosing are of good quality, with healthy foliage and strong stems, so that they will give you a beautiful display for the maximum amount of time. This is particularly important with very simple arrangements, when the flowers really have to speak for themselves.

• Flowers which are in bud when bought or harvested from the garden will give the longest display and will also give you the pleasure of watching them come into full bloom. Commercially grown flowers are usually specially treated to prolong their lifespan. Most fresh flowers should last five days or more and those available in supermarkets are often guaranteed to bloom for a certain number of days.

• If you're buying flowers from a florist, don't be afraid to ask for advice – they ought to be knowledgeable about their stock and happy to help with any queries you may have.

• If you're cutting flowers from your own garden, carry a container of water around with you into which you can immediately plunge the cut stems. This will prevent them drying out before you get them inside and into their own vase or container.

• Remember that with annual flowers, the more you harvest them, the more blooms they'll produce, so don't be afraid to cut them regularly. You may even want to grow some plants specially for arrangements in the house. If you're an inexperienced gardener, choose packets of seed labelled 'hardy annual', which can be sowed straight into the soil following the instructions on the packet.

• When you get your cut flowers home, take at least 1cm (½in) off the bottom of the stems with a pair of sharp scissors or secateurs, cut on an angle to help maximize their absorption of water.

• Before arranging your flowers, give them a good, long drink in deep water to firm up the stems and help them to last longer – they'll absorb half the water they need in the first 24 hours.

• Most bought bunches of flowers come with a sachet of plant food. It's well worth using and will prolong the life of your flowers. If you're using plants from the garden, florists also suggest adding sugar, lemonade or aspirin to the water to keep your flowers looking healthy for longer.

• If you're using material with woody stems, such as branches of blossom, smash the ends with a hammer or rolling pin to help them to take up water.

• If you're using carnations, cut them just above a leaf nodule.

• Leave daffodils in water overnight to remove excess sap before arranging.

• If you're using Iceland poppies, leave the stems uncut or, if you cut them, singe the ends with a match or on a gas hob. Otherwise they'll exude a milky sap.

• Strip stems of leaves where they'll be below the water line or they'll become slimy and cloud the water. In any case, it's a good idea to remove some of the leaves so that they're not competing with the stems for water.

• Use tepid water in which to arrange your flowers because oxygen travels more readily through warm water, and therefore up the plant's stems, than it does through cold water.

• Some cut flowers, such as gerberas, love-lies-bleeding and dill, benefit from having their stems plunged into boiling water before being arranged.

• Some flowers, such as violets, are less likely to flag if they are submerged in cool water overnight before being arranged. You can keep them looking fresh by spritzing the arrangement frequently with cold water.

• To maximize the life of your flowers, keep the water crystal clear. This means changing the water regularly – probably every other day – and keeping your containers squeaky clean.

• Some of the longest lasting flowers are chrysanthemums, carnations, hydrangeas, roses and calla lilies. Dahlias, sweet peas and anemones are among those which don't last as well.

• To keep your arrangement looking good, remove dead flower heads and leaves when they appear.

• Think twice about displaying tulips in a mixed arrangement. The acidity in tulips can shorten the life of other blooms.

• If you're arranging scented flowers they'll release their perfume better in a warm room than a cold one.

• Tropical leaves often have a sticky sap on their surface which you can remove by wiping them or dipping them in water.

• If you're using lilies, remove the stamens to prevent their pollen staining anything.

index

suppliers

Vases and Containers

The Conran Shop
Michelin House
81 Fulham Road
London SW3 6RD
020 7589 7401
www.conran.co.uk
Selection of cutting-edge designs.

Designer's Guild
Includes architectural vases designed
by Christian Tortu.
020 7351 5775 for stockists or
0845 6021189 for mail order.
www.designersguild.com

Habitat
196 Tottenham Court Road
London W1T 9LD
0845 601 0740
www.habitat.net
Wide range of metal, wooden and
glass vases. Also sells galvanized
florist's buckets.

Heal's
196 Tottenham Court Road
London W1T 7LQ
020 7636 1666
www.heals.co.uk
Cool and classic vases.

John Lewis
Oxford Street
London W1A 1EX
020 7629 7711
And branches nationwide.
www.johnlewis.com
A good range of affordable vases.

LSA International
www.lsa-international.co.uk
Contemporary homewares brand
which includes glass and porcelain
vases. Stocked by a wide variety of
retailers, from department stores
to boutiques.
Call 01932 789721 for stockists.

Mint
70 Wigmore St
London W1U 2SQ
020 7224 4406
Rubber vases.

Models Own
2 Fairfax Place
Dartmouth
Devon TQ6 9AD
0800 169 9228
www.modelsown.com
Modern, retro- and country-style vases.

OKA
Tower Road
Berinsfield
Nr. Abingdon
OX10 7LN
0870 160 6002
www.okadirect.com
Good for bamboo-shaped vases.

Purves and Purves
220–224 Tottenham Court Road
London W1T 7QE
020 7580 8223
www.purves.co.uk
Stock includes bright plastic vases.

Selfridges
400 Oxford Street
London W1A 1AB
020 7629 1234
&
1 The Dome
The Trafford Centre
Manchester M17 8DA
0161 6291234
www.selfridges.co.uk
Designer accessories from around
the world.

Skandium
72 Wigmore Street
London W1H 9DL
020 7935 2077
www.skandium.com
Modern Scandinavian designs.

Flower Markets

Covent Garden Market
Nine Elms
London SW8 5NX

Columbia Road Flower Market
Columbia Road
London E2 7QB
Sundays 08.00–14.00

Horticultural Market
Pershore Street
Birmingham B5
0121 622 4111

Gateway House
Bernard Street
Southampton SO14 2NS
023 8022 1212

New Smithfield Market
Whitworth Street East
Openshaw
Manchester M11 2WJ
0161 223 9036/9639

Yorkshire Produce Centre
Pontefract Lane
Leeds LS9 0PS
0113 201 9888

To find retail florists in your area, go to the
Flowers and Plants Association website at:
www.flowers.org